Glyn Davis AC is CEO of the Paul Ramsay Foundation, which works to end intergenerational poverty. He was previously Vice-Chancellor of the University of Melbourne and remains Distinguished Professor of Political Science at the Australian National University and visiting Professor at the Blavatnik School of Government, Oxford. He delivered the Boyer Lectures on the future of higher education in 2010.

Writers in the *On Series*

Glyn Davis

On Life's Lottery

hachette
AUSTRALIA

hachette
AUSTRALIA

Published in Australia and New Zealand in 2021
by Hachette Australia
(an imprint of Hachette Australia Pty Limited)
Level 17, 207 Kent Street, Sydney NSW 2000
www.hachette.com.au

10 9 8 7 6 5 4 3 2 1

 A catalogue record for this
book is available from the
NATIONAL LIBRARY OF AUSTRALIA   National Library of Australia

ISBN: 978 0 7336 4651 5 (paperback)

Cover design by Luke Causby, Blue Cork
Text design by Alice Graphics
Typeset by Kirby Jones
Printed and bound in Great Britain by Clays Ltd, Elcograf S.p.A.

 The paper this book is printed on is
certified against the Forest Stewardship
Council® Standards. McPherson's Printing
Group holds FSC® chain of custody
certification SA-COC-005379. FSC® promotes environmentally
responsible, socially beneficial and economically viable
management of the world's forests.

We find ourselves in the city of Omelas, 'bright-towered by the sea'. The bayside setting is beautiful, the citizens lithe and carefree, the political system simple and accommodating. There are no kings, no slaves, just happy people. As the short story opens, the city begins its annual Festival of Summer.

Yet there is a price for such shared joy. In a basement beneath one building is a locked door leading to a room with no window.

Trapped within is a small distressed child, neglected, shunned and squatting on a dirt floor. Occasionally the door opens and people stand briefly on the threshold, staring with 'frightened, disgusted eyes' at the child. Hastily, the food bowl and water jug are refilled, the door locked and darkness restored.

Every person in Omelas knows about the locked door and its prisoner; many will visit while still young and find themselves sickened by the sight. They understand that the wealth and prosperity of their city depends on maintaining the child's 'abominable misery'. Some would like to help but feel powerless. They know Omelas would fall if the child was released, cleaned and given back its life.

These are the terms for a rich and fulfilled existence in Omelas. Whatever their private qualms, most people accept the bitter injustice that one must suffer so everyone else can be happy. For a handful, though, the knowledge becomes unbearable. Always alone, a woman or man will quietly leave the city and keep travelling, ever further into the darkness.

In 'The Ones Who Walk Away from Omelas', novelist and poet Ursula Le Guin asks what suffering we will accept in return for social harmony. Implicit is a very personal question: are we the idealists who cannot endure rough treatment for a stranger and flee, or the pragmatists who find a way to live with our guilty conscience so most people can thrive? The choices made by the citizens of Omelas are conscious and deliberate, even if quickly put out of mind.

Le Guin reminds us that birth is the great gamble. She points to the strange calculus at its core. In life we take a ticket and are born into families, health, genders, ethnicities and societies we do not choose. We may be a fulfilled citizen or the child in the basement.

Birth is a throw of the dice. The consequences can last a lifetime. If you believe people deserve an equal chance to prosper, this game of chance is deeply disturbing if nothing follows to even up the inherent unfairness.

My brothers and I were blessed, born into a loving family. We were encouraged, supported, nurtured. Our parents live still by a profound faith that frames their ethics, makes them trusting, generous to others, charitable, understanding, forgiving of human flaws. Such good fortune reflects no merit on our part, just the lottery at work.

Begin in a modestly prosperous family and life, by and large, can be good. Be a neglected child – or the child of a neglected child – and the shadow may fall over every aspect of your existence and stalk the next generation. Get sick, flee war, be deprived of education, suffer discrimination, have your land appropriated by settlers and the odds are stacked against you.

Chance shapes us. We find the right partner, win an unexpected election and life hurtles in a new and exciting direction. Or an obscure coronavirus mutates, a long boom ends brutally and millions are thrown into unemployment. Our existence is not linear.

As the economist Robert H. Frank argues, luck plays 'a much larger role in important life outcomes' than most people imagine. 'There, but for an accident of birth, or the grace of God, or the mystery of fate, go I,' philosopher Michael Sandel reminds us.

This inescapable lottery poses a moral question. Birth is always a gamble but must the life that follows be tied to the same game of chance?

There are millions of Australians who believe good fortune carries a responsibility to help those facing difficulty. Some 80 per cent of adult Australians make charitable donations each year, and many invest their time helping charities and other community organisations such as schools.

Volunteers with the Salvation Army work in the charity's stores, provide legal services, and undertake street work with the homeless and young people in distress. They fan out across Australia for the annual Red Shield Appeal. Many charitable services would not be possible without these big-hearted Australians. The Salvation Army describes such work as the 'everyday embodiment of love in action'.

As my brothers and I grew up, we watched our parents volunteer year after year at the St Vincent de Paul Society. They told us little at the time, but reminisced later in life about what must have proved a sometimes wrenching experience.

Like many charities, Vinnies received endless appeals for support. Since the charity could not meet demand, nor afford many paid staff, volunteers would be asked to visit and assess, sympathetically, the need in a distressed household.

The chain began in the local Vinnies shop, where my mother worked with like-minded volunteers sorting donations of clothes, furniture and toys into piles to give away or sell.

Money made in the shop would fund vouchers. These my parents carried with them on home visits in response to requests for help. Decades later, my father can still describe in detail the empty fridges, the cold houses, the distraught migrants and the abandoned wives with no money and young children to feed.

The assistance offered felt inadequate though essential. And charity carried a sting – the vouchers, redeemable at a local supermarket, were clearly marked: 'Not to be used for alcohol.'

Here was poverty stark and immediate with charity unable to do more than respond to the urgent.

As a graduate student at the Australian National University I joined a college program to distribute meals on wheels. In wealthy Canberra I thought there may be few takers. The long Saturdays collecting hot food and driving it to grateful people proved otherwise. Those we served were usually old, struggling on a pension, and sometimes fearful about keeping their small apartment as bills overwhelmed meagre finances.

All lived frugal lives. Many were lonely. They felt cast out, telling stories that under-lined isolation. They had drifted to the national capital for work or relationships and later found themselves alone with nowhere to go, no place where they belonged. Here was hunger for company and meaning, when all we could offer was an ear and warm food in a plastic tub covered with silver foil.

As volunteers we glimpsed only fleetingly something profound about the loss of social capital for those without resources. The experience left me with abiding admiration for people who dedicate their lives to helping others. Working with the elderly stressed the importance of this work but also the value of early opportunity. As Conny Lenneberg,

Executive Director of the Brotherhood of St Laurence, expressed it recently: 'You mitigate poverty with older groups but you find pathways out of poverty for children and youth.'

How common is such deprivation in our midst? We hope that hard work, determination and talent will allow people to find their way in the world. Draw the right ticket in the lottery and this is often true. Yet the scale of disadvantage in our community is confronting. Some 3.24 million Australians live below the poverty line according to *Poverty in Australia 2020*, a report compiled before the economic downturn triggered by the COVID-19 pandemic. This represents slightly more than 13 per cent of the population, including three quarters of a million children.

Despite our image of Australia as the land of the fair go, our levels of poverty are slightly higher than OECD averages. The rate fluctuates year to year but has remained close to current levels for at least a decade. The high cost of housing, declining incomes and the low level of social security benefits are key drivers.

Single parents, recent migrants, Australians living alone or outside a major urban area, people emerging from the criminal justice system, those less qualified, and people on social security benefits, such as the elderly, are particularly at risk. Disability has been a persistent marker of disadvantage, linked to limited employment opportunities and transport options.

Above all, Aboriginal and Torres Strait Islander Australians face poverty levels almost double that experienced by other Australians. As a June 2019 study from the ANU reported: 'Indigenous citizens are still far from equal participants in Australian society … they are deeply disadvantaged across a vast array of indicators.'

To express poverty in statistics conveys little of the lived reality. A static picture provides no feel for the patterns which play out in Australia.

So, let's start from a different point: if you are born into one of the poorest households in Australia, what are your chances of breaking out, of achieving a more prosperous life as adults? Can we predict likely outcomes for those young children in distressed households visited by my parents?

Following decades of detailed survey work, we know the answer. It is dispiriting. Studies by the Melbourne Institute confirm that children born into disadvantage struggle to break out of disadvantage in adulthood.

On average, the more years a child spends in poverty, the worse their socio-economic outcomes. Children from poor households are more likely to experience mental and physical health challenges. Many will struggle to complete education or compete in the labour market. A child from an impoverished background is five times more likely to suffer adult poverty and two and half times more likely to need social housing. A 2016 Productivity Commission report on deep disadvantage identified a similar pattern, with around half those afflicted by poverty trapped in disadvantage for long periods.

As Australians we pride ourselves on being a meritocratic society, but the success of a few can hide the underlying truth: entrenched intergenerational poverty, like the property of the wealthy, is handed down from parent to child. For the poorest in our society, social mobility is highly constrained. Each time the lottery plays, the same results emerge. Most will do well but for more than one in ten Australians a lifetime of economic struggle beckons.

It is easy to look away, to accept the world as we find it. The early economist Thomas Malthus wrote 'that from the inevitable laws of our nature some human beings must suffer from want. These are the unhappy persons who, in the great lottery of life, have drawn a blank'.

What Malthus accepted as an inevitable reality – the unhappy destiny of the child in Omelas – others contest. For how we respond to misfortune in our society speaks to our most profound moral, philosophical and political beliefs. It is a central question of life: what are our obligations to others?

In his 2012 essay 'Ethics and Poverty' philosopher Peter Singer argues we have an obligation to assist. If we encounter a child drowning, we should put aside concern for our clothes and shoes and swim to the rescue, because the harm we can avert is so much more important than the cost to ourselves.

Singer expresses this as a simple principle: 'If it is in our power to prevent something very bad happening, without thereby sacrificing anything of comparable moral importance, we ought, morally, to do it.'

The caveat about 'comparable moral importance' is significant. Our obligation to others is not an absolute moral imperative which overrides all other considerations, but a judgement about consequences. If responding requires us to be unjust to others, or to accept an unreasonable burden, then the calculation shifts. But if the cost is small in comparison to the difference we can make, our responsibility is clear.

Singer believes the requirement to assist applies 'not just to rare situations in which one can save a child from a pond, but to the everyday situation in which we can assist those living in extreme poverty'. If an affluent society can help, it should. This is not about charity but a moral obligation, 'something that everyone ought to do'.

In Omelas, helping the child would end prosperity. This leaves the citizens ambivalent. They know the price matters when weighing moral challenges.

Peter Singer presents the imperative to address poverty as a matter of ethics, yet our world is shaped also by politics. I was in Canberra to write a doctoral thesis in political science. It seemed the ideal place to study the national story up close: the intricate dance between principle and pragmatism that is political life. Yet, if poverty endured just a short bus ride from Parliament House, what did this say about Australian attitudes to addressing misfortune?

We can tell the Australian story in different ways. One narrative would stress a record of innovation in caring for others. The Commonwealth of Australia, created in 1901, acted quickly to introduce a basic living wage and social security. National senior and invalid pensions began in 1909, building on earlier state schemes and learning from Germany, Denmark and New Zealand. The arbitration system ensured workers could support a family. Unemployment benefits followed after World War I, along with pensions for veterans, support for mothers and children, and access to health support.

As sociologist Sian Supski notes, when politicians ran out of money to pay for these schemes, they licenced state lotteries which distributed profits to charities, so adding to social services.

However, the Australian settlement never pursued radical redistribution of wealth. An alternative reading would observe that social benefit payments remain modest, and usually means tested. This leaves many Australians to grow up in poverty. For decades, the electorate has chosen governments which are slightly more taxing and spending than the United States but significantly less committed to social security than Europeans.

In the OECD world, Australia sits among the bottom third of member nations ranked for taxes and government expenditure with commensurately constrained support for the poor.

This preference is reflected in electoral outcomes. One side of politics has dominated the Australian federal parliament over the past three generations, with the Coalition and its predecessors governing for almost 60 of the 90 years since the Great Depression.

Such consistent electoral success suggests an enduring consensus on what voters will surrender to assist others. Almost every Australian election is a referendum on how much tax people are willing to pay and the answer is usually the same.

As a consequence, there are limits to public largesse. This leaves a large gap for charity to fill. In return, government licences charities and rewards donors through tax exemptions, giving up public revenue in return for social provision by private effort. Our politics assume that mitigating life's lottery is not solely a matter for government.

Charities appeared early in Australia, long before democratic institutions or public welfare programs. The Benevolent Society, Australia's oldest charity, began in 1813 to help distressed families, the elderly and people with disability. Eliza Darling launched the Female Friendly Society in 1826. Much early charity was inspired by religious devotion. Caroline Chisholm worked tirelessly to assist homeless immigrants, and is now listed as a saint by the Church of England.

The nineteenth century proved a period for vibrant private initiatives, self-help mutual societies, and the origins of many significant charities. The St Vincent de Paul Society began in Australia in 1854, the local chapter of the Salvation Army in 1881. Following Federation, the Australian Red Cross opened in 1914, the Smith Family in 1922 and the Brotherhood of St Laurence in 1930.

Alongside charities is a lesser known form of philanthropy: foundations which exist solely to fund the work of others. This tradition dates back to 1886 when Dr William Wyatt, through his will, created an organisation to support South Australians experiencing hardship. The Paul Ramsay Foundation is the largest addition to the Australian network of foundations, supporting charities committed to ending intergenerational poverty.

Through donations, Australians each year contribute more than $12.5 billion to supporting everything from child protection and emergency relief to programs for refugees. Business is active too, contributing a further $17.5 billion annually in charitable donations. Collectively we support some 56,000 registered not-for-profit organisations across the nation.

This generosity supports a large and expanding charitable sector, employing more than 1.3 million Australians part and full-time. Many services once delivered by public servants are now contracted to for-purpose organisations, blurring the line between the obligations of the state and the voluntary labour of charity.

Yet, apparently impressive figures can mislead. Overall, charitable spending remains small compared to government. Combined state and federal spending on education, health and welfare dwarfs resources available to charities. Rarely does charity alone have the financial heft to lift people from poverty. Government remains the most significant player in addressing disadvantage.

So charity alone cannot offset the lottery of life, however vital the work as benefactor and friend of those in distress. In an earlier Australia, charity dominated provision of support to people afflicted by misfortune. Now Australians look to government for pensions and welfare payments. Such services require the scale and reach of the state but do not meet all deprivation in society. The charitable sector sits around the edges of public investment, its terrain defined by public programs. Charity needs to be where government chose to be absent.

For some, any remaining role is an indictment of our society.

'Charity', British Labour Prime Minister Clement Attlee reputedly said, 'is a cold grey loveless thing. If a rich man wants to help the poor, he should pay his taxes gladly, not dole out money at a whim.'

Attlee believed that public policy, funded by appropriate levels of taxation, is the most effective way to address disadvantage. Government can be universal, while charity is not democratic. Only government, Attlee argued, can address causes and not just symptoms of social problems.

The welfare state he championed changed Britain. The National Health Scheme remains its most enduring institution, applauded every night by Conservative Prime Minister Boris Johnson during the COVID-19 pandemic.

Australia did not accept with the same enthusiasm either the diagnosis or the proposed solution. The local welfare state introduced after World War II was never as far reaching, nor as universal as in Britain. It did, though, achieve some notable successes. Medicare and related public health initiatives, early childhood services, the higher education contribution scheme and, despite its teething challenges, the National Disability Insurance Scheme all remove some financial barriers to fuller participation in community life. We are a more equitable society as a result.

Yet government often struggles to achieve nuanced service delivery. The conspicuous failure of the 'Close the Gap' program, designed to eliminate differences in health outcomes and life expectancy for Aboriginal and Torres Strait Islander Australians, offers the signature example. As the Australian Human Rights Commission noted, this most pressing and enduring national emergency has been a tale of disappointment, leaving a generation without the public health outcomes promised by government and opposition alike. A 2020 reboot seeks to get the program back on track but it will remain a challenge to close the gap, as committed, by 2030.

Noel Pearson has described poor design and delivery of government services as leading to 'passive welfare' – programs that accentuate the problem they seek to solve and so condemn recipients to inequality through dependence on public payments. Marcia Langton argues that economic inclusion, not a 'state-imposed tangle of policies, programs and bureaucracy' is required urgently.

The result can be an impasse with complex social problems unaddressed as charities lack the money, and governments lack the appropriate design, local engagement and commitment to quality service delivery.

This leaves many Australians mired in intergenerational disadvantage.

Bob Hawke promised to end child poverty by 1990, yet there are still 739,000 Australian children living below the poverty line. Malcolm Turnbull committed to 'reduce by at least half the proportion of men, women and children living in poverty in all its dimensions', but the numbers remain stubbornly unmoved. Despite goodwill and significant public expenditure, misfortune persists.

Poverty constrains the ability of people to shape their own lives. A cycle that begins before birth can play out through life, ensuring that poverty begets poverty. The accumulation of setbacks experienced by many young people prevents them finding a way to better economic circumstances for themselves and, one day, their own children.

Yet there is reason for quiet optimism. Some promising initiatives seek to redraw the separation between government and charity. What if communities and government agencies, charities and foundations could combine their intelligence and resources around an agreed goal?

Two examples show such collaboration in practice: one helping children prepare for and succeed in school; the other seeking to keep young people out of jail. In each case the collaboration addresses a cycle of disadvantage, a trap that leaves people otherwise unable to escape the cumulative effects of setback and disadvantage.

Numerous charities work hard to break the cycle for children, offering maternal screening, child and family health nursing, parenting programs, community services for young families, playgroups, long day care and specialist preschool offerings.

Each offers an 'off-ramp' (to use the expression proposed by Dr Jeni Whalan at the Paul Ramsay Foundation), which is a targeted intervention to help a child avoid poverty. Cycles of disadvantage have strong and weak points: on-ramps where the flow of disadvantage is increased but also potential off-ramps that offer an opportunity to escape the endless repetition that confronts so many in endemic poverty. Diagnosis of a cycle can identify points of intervention and encourage better program design. Inevitably, this requires an individual approach. As people who work in early childhood always stress, there is no single solution to a challenge such as school readiness. Every child is different; every disadvantaged family lives with disadvantage in its own way.

Since many factors push people into a cycle, many different off-ramps are required. Governments provide important services but the task can be daunting for agencies which must deploy standardised approaches. Charities do not have the same resources but can work closely with families and tailor appropriate programs.

Put the two approaches together and new possibilities open. In an ideal setting, pre-school and education support, health services and transition to work programs, public and private, would all be linked so a child at risk has encouragement and support all the way through to adult life. Such an integrated service would work locally so individual needs and aspirations can be heard.

This is the approach adopted by Our Place, a Victorian initiative which began at Doveton College in 2012 and now extends to ten sites across the state. Using the local primary school as the site, Our Place integrates service delivery for children and their families in disadvantaged communities. It has inspired relevant government departments to pool their expertise. A ten year commitment from the Colman Foundation made the project possible and now others fund projects across the Our Place network.

A recently opened but typical Our Place facility involves a partnership between the Carlton Primary School, the City of Melbourne and the Carlton housing estate. The school sits adjacent to public housing, a pocket of disadvantage in an otherwise affluent suburb. Only two per cent of students at the school come from English speaking backgrounds.

This is a linguistically and culturally diverse gathering of migrants and refugees in one community, sharing ageing buildings which were locked down – with the residents inside – during COVID-19. Notable investment by the state government includes a former school building refurbished to provide education facilities, an early learning service, community spaces, health consulting rooms, and a mother and childcare service. Gowrie Victoria has joined to operate the early learning centre, while the YMCA offers after school activities, all coordinated by a dedicated community facilitator.

The Our Place model argues that programs should focus not just on children but also on their families. Therefore attention is also paid to adult education, recognising that getting unemployed parents into work brings broader benefits for their children. Our Place calls this 'reshaping the service system' to provide wrap-around support.

Underpinning the specifics of the program is a large ambition: to lift an entire community from deep disadvantage. Doveton College, where the project began, is located in a suburb developed by the Victorian Housing Commission from the 1950s around large automobile, machinery and food processing plants on the outskirts of Melbourne. For thirty glorious years the new community flourished but then the factories began to close. By 2015 unemployment in the suburb was 21.1 per cent, four times the Australian average. With the lack of work came a raft of social problems.

As one of the few functioning institutions in a troubled suburb, Doveton College decided its young students needed a dedicated program so they could thrive despite a bleak context. Our Place was born.

A 2020 evaluation by Dr Dennis Glover – himself the son of local factory workers and a graduate of Doveton College – found much to celebrate. The integrated programs pioneered at Doveton, with results carefully measured, have made a difference. Children at the school show increased ability to learn and lower developmental vulnerability. Student absenteeism has fallen and academic results improved.

Parental involvement has grown with more fathers and mothers reading to their children. Parents are studying, enrolling in vocational training. Local unemployment has fallen as newly trained adults find jobs and median family income rises. With more prosperity, youth crime rates have declined.

Dr Glover does not downplay the difficulties which buffet Doveton still. Ironically, the success of the program, along with changing demographics, has encouraged more affluent families to move in, creating affordability challenges for older residents. Nonetheless, the evaluation demonstrates how coordinating government and charitable services around shared goals, using the local school as the hub, makes a measurable and sustained contribution to community wellbeing. Keeping young people engaged in education offers opportunity. Helping parents acquire skills – and jobs – allows Doveton to become more than 'another struggling community.'

A second example of collaboration addresses a very different cycle of disadvantage. There are 77,000 Australian children with parents currently in prison. Too many are from Aboriginal and Torres Strait Islander families, the most incarcerated peoples in the world. Indeed, a 2017 report by PWC Indigenous Consulting found that 'an estimated 20 per cent of Indigenous children have at least one parent in prison at any time' – a profoundly shocking statistic.

Children with parents in jail are among those Australians most likely also to suffer financial hardship and developmental challenges. Most people in jail have led disadvantaged lives. Alongside a higher risk of prison, poverty can mean poor health and wellbeing, incomplete high school education and, in time, a risk that children will repeat the cycle experienced by their parents.

Here is intergenerational transmission of disadvantage at its most stark. A *majority* of Australians in custody are the child of a parent jailed in the past.

This burden is felt acutely by young Aboriginal and Torres Strait Islander people. The *Bringing Them Back Home* report dedicated much needed attention to juvenile justice. For many, early encounters with authority become 'the start of a long career of incarceration'.

For one community, enough was enough. The Maranguka Justice Reinvestment project in Bourke in far-west New South Wales challenges a long-established pattern. The Maranguka project strives to end the incarceration of young Aboriginal women and men, and with it the intergenerational trauma of early encounters with the justice system.

Bourke has a complex history, beginning as a stockade on Ngemba lands amid frontier clashes between traditional owners and new settlers. The town later attracted many displaced Aboriginal people as cattle and sheep came to dominate the landscape. Employment proved hard to find. For a long time Bourke held the dubious distinction of the highest conviction rate for Aboriginal youth under 17 in New South Wales.

Sentencing did little to change behaviour – 90 per cent of young people released from custody were in trouble with the law once again within a year.

Local Aboriginal leaders decided it was past time to end the cycle of children taken from families, youth crime, and high rates of imprisonment. Activists such as Alistair Ferguson looked for inspiration to justice reinvestment programs in the United States, which urge government to keep people out of prison, and invest the considerable savings in the community.

As the Australian Law Reform Commission observes, the justice reinvestment model sees prisons as a policy failure, an expensive option that achieves little for community or those incarcerated. Better to 'reduce criminality at source through investment in social justice'.

In this spirit a coalition of Aboriginal leaders, law reform advocates, professional service firms and foundations agreed to work together on a plan for Bourke.

Eventually the collaboration reached out to government, and NSW Health Minister Brad Hazzard became the 'cross sector champion', ensuring public agencies worked in a coordinated way. As the Minister told a public meeting in Bourke: 'I still shake my head in wonder as to why so much state and federal resources are coming into regional towns and not achieving the outcomes we want.'

The Maranguka approach empowers individuals. The intervention can be simple, such as supporting people to get birth certificates so they can access services (an estimated 200,000 Aboriginal and Torres Strait Islander people lack this basic documentation). In Bourke, an early win was teaching Aboriginal youth to drive and obtain licences, which requires a birth certificate. Some 236 young people accepted the challenge, so reducing a common source of conflict with local police.

Attention then turned to ambitious further targets: alternatives for young people to avoid offending, broader options around sentencing and initiatives to reduce reoffending. Aboriginal leaders urged the Maranguka project team to look unflinchingly at causes alongside solutions. This required difficult conversations around every marker of disadvantage: 'early life, education, employment, housing, healthcare, child safety, and health outcomes including mental health and drugs and alcohol'.

Often answers involved working with authorities but sometimes change was needed closer to home. The Men of Bourke group confronted the high rates of domestic violence in the community. A Men's Space, built on the site of an old prison, became a symbol of taking ownership. As Robert Milliken observes in his impressive report on the Maranguka project for *Inside Story*, the proportion of adult men charged with domestic violence subsequently fell by almost half.

To lead the Bourke initiative, two new organisations were created under Aboriginal leadership. These are the spine of the project, called Maranguka ('caring for others' in the Ngemba language), and the Bourke Tribal Council, a broader body which represents the twenty-two language groups in the town. Nested within these arrangements are many community groups, including youth-led organisations which work with young people at risk of offending.

Reaching out to the police took time, with much mutual distrust to address first. But once established, the links allow for a conversation every morning between police and youth workers about what happened in the town overnight, whether young people are in trouble, and how they might be encouraged to return to school. A youth council advises the project and liaises with school principals and officials from the Bourke Shire Council.

Here is a significant departure from tradi-tional patterns of service delivery. Community sets the agenda, authority is shared, and charities become part of the policy process, not just a means of distributing aid.

As at Doveton, the evaluation to date is promising. Nearly a third more students are completing Year 12 in Bourke and juvenile offences have fallen by a similar amount. Days spent in custody declined by nearly half. An assessment by KPMG suggests improved justice outcomes should save around $7 million over five years in Bourke – money to reinvest in the community.

Just as Our Place grew from Doveton to a state-wide initiative, so the Just Reinvest movement sees a role for similar programs in other communities struggling with incarceration. When a fundraising campaign was launched at Government House in Sydney, then fifteen-year-old Trei Stewart spoke to the NSW Governor, Premier, Attorney-General and community leaders.

A Yuin Nation man, Trei described a troubled childhood, which saw him taken from his family by government officials.

Trei eventually found a sense of belonging by moving in with his grandparents and joining the local Kool Kids Club. His aspirations changed: to finish high school, find a meaningful job and raise a family of his own.

'The money that builds the walls to hold us in', he said, 'could be better spent.' Being locked up destroys hopes for the future. Trei concluded with a plea – we want 'to be not just another statistic. All we want is a chance. Allow us to have that chance'.

Trei's life continues to present challenges. He has written about his subsequent struggles with mental health, noting that suicide is the leading cause of death for Aboriginal and Torres Strait Islander people under the age of 35. Now a young adult, Trei serves as a Youth Ambassador for programs to stop building prisons and instead address the causes of disadvantage.

In Doveton, and in Bourke, well-led partnerships transform lives. A collaborative approach expands choices and opportunities for individuals. It gives young people tangible options and demonstrates that others care about their journey.

This collaborative approach for communities has a name: collective impact. It assumes coordinated work among government and for-purpose organisations towards a shared goal has a better chance of success than isolated pursuit by a single government agency or mission-driven charity. Collective impact requires a common agenda, a shared measurement system, mutually reinforcing activities, continuous dialogue and a backbone organisation.

The collective impact movement is now well established with manuals, guidebooks and an accepted sequence for implementation. Since every innovation generates critics there is also a lively counter-narrative, and the prospect therefore of learning and improvement. Debate and evaluation ensure the founding ideas have evolved over time, finding better ways towards systemic change through a focus on place and community.

Collective work imposes uncomfortable demands on everyone. Communities are asked to take ownership of local problems. Government agencies are expected to collaborate, pool funding, and work to priorities set by the project. Local business must accept a role in securing outcomes for the neighbourhood. Collective impact demands charities and foundations be patient while community leaders and their public agency partners experiment, fail, and then fail better.

It is hard for government to delegate the control of expenditure, or to share risk if something goes badly wrong. It is challenging too for charities to fund programs when they must hand leadership to others. Yet the model now has an established history across Australia with programs such as the Cape York Partnerships program, the eight empowered urban, regional and remote Aboriginal and Torres Strait Islander communities and emerging place-based initiatives including Logan Together in south-east Queensland, and the Hive at Mt Druitt in Sydney and Brimbank in the north-west of Melbourne.

Each targets a different cycle of disadvantage, measuring change and building expertise on what works. Together they point to an effective way to address disadvantage through a process that begins with community voice.

In Britain, the collective impact model jostles uncomfortably with the universal provision of Attlee's welfare state. As Hilary Cottam explains in her influential book *Radical Help*, British government agencies struggle with the shift from delivering top-down programs to developing and delivering programs in partnership with those they seek to support. Yet to succeed interventions must place people at the centre of services and not be afraid to remain narrow. Not every initiative needs scale or national consistency.

Change becomes possible when government agencies are willing to work as equals with individuals, communities, charities, businesses and foundations. As Pamela Ryan observed, the best aid does not look like aid. It looks like, and is, collaboration. Responses are 'best enacted by local organisations who are resourced (with skills, knowledge, networks, funding and other materials) to do the immediate job and build capacity for the long term.'

If poverty was easy to solve, it would not long endure. That it persists despite much public and private investment, despite people and agencies committed to its eradication, despite generations of social science research and policy proposals, points to the implausibility of swift solutions. The most promising initiatives are also the most time consuming. Collective impact involves long timelines and endless perseverance to work through each cycle of disadvantage, understand it, and create new off-ramps.

Yet strive we must. Our obligation does not diminish because the task is hard. The persistence of inequality should leave few illusions about the structural nature of disadvantage. It is not only a matter of funding but of acknowledging and addressing racism, isolation and cultural barriers.

For some people requiring Meals on Wheels in Canberra, mental health and disability proved formidable barriers to participation. They could not find a way into community. A shared life must be more than modest social benefits delivered anonymously to a bank account, or a Saturday afternoon visit from a student bearing a chicken stew.

People are inventive and independent. Give them a viable off-ramp and they will take control of their lives. Yet *Two Australias: a report on poverty in the land of plenty* suggested that for people left out 'choices are few and deprivations are many'. Those living with disadvantage 'do not want charity' said the authors. 'They want justice. They want fairness.'

Cycles of disadvantage are dogged and entrenched but not impervious. Our world can prove more malleable than expected. Just as our childhood seems inevitable, a time when everything is fixed and preordained, so social arrangements appear immutable. Debates about the right level of social provision in Australia rumble on for decades with little change in outcomes.

And then society is upended. COVID-19 arrives and governments suddenly experiment with a universal basic income, free childcare, doubled social security payments, hotel accom-modation for people living on the streets, guarantees of employment, and a moratorium on rent payment and eviction. Emergency payments briefly lift some relying on Commonwealth benefits above the poverty line.

These innovations also underscored a sharp line in our society: those eligible for support, and the refugees, recent migrants and stranded international students deemed as not meriting public assistance.

For many Australians, the recession that has followed COVID-19 has up-ended a sense of security.

'As they age and succeed,' says author Michael Lewis, 'people feel their success was somehow inevitable. They don't want to acknowledge the role played by accident in their lives.'

So, to be suddenly at the mercy of impersonal economics has been sobering. The pandemic revealed the fragility of many people, businesses and social institutions. It also demonstrated the strength of community, a stoicism to endure, fortitude amid adversity. Most Australians accepted social isolation for months at a stretch because they acknowledged the risk to others from spreading infection.

Their leaders also rose to the challenge. COVID-19 upturned decades of conventional thinking about the use of public funds. Citizens welcomed a federal government working closely with states to co-ordinate care and support: a brief vision of a different, more collaborative, Australia.

Let this prove more than a flash of summer lightning. Governments and communities, working together, can manage adversity through sharing power. The lowest interest rates in history offer a chance to rethink public investment. A nation that saves its people from calamitous health outcomes and deploys vast reserves to soften economic distress can also address poverty.

To do so, government must engage more effectively with charities. Charities can help those most at disadvantage but cannot solve problems alone; the imbalance in resources requires partnership. Pressing elected representatives should be part of the philanthropic enterprise. Charity must not be silent about advocating for greater fairness, even when this offends politicians. 'Advancing public debate' is an acceptable objective under charities legislation.

It is not enough to give: the challenge is to empower by addressing the causes of poverty. Inevitably this is a political argument.

Australians show little inclination to embrace the Attlee approach to welfare, so our past will likely also be our future: a combination of public and private spending to address disadvantage. But assistance can be made more effective as charities join government and community in analysis and response to the causes of poverty.

Greater methodological sophistication will help direct investment. Random-controlled trials, familiar from medicine, test whether investment in an off-ramp achieves its objectives. The Smith Family is measuring the effectiveness of early childhood interventions through careful study. The Brotherhood of St Laurence is using a fidelity model test to understand how variation in program design and delivery affect results in securing employment for young people.

In *Randomistas*, economist and Shadow Assistant Treasurer Andrew Leigh argues for a 'what works' approach to social policy, informed by rigorous evaluation. He commends the informal motto of the British Cabinet Office: 'Test. Learn. Adapt.'

Improved data sources and information technology can also focus investment. When charities respond to bushfire they draw on new visualisation tools. These map the geography of fire damage, and then overlay Department of Social Services data showing income distribution before a fire and insurance claims afterwards. Such information helps pinpoint areas of acute need and track long-term changes resulting from disaster. The data are all in the public domain.

The for-purpose sector has also grown in ambition. Alongside well-established social enterprises such as the Vinnies op shops are commercial instruments to achieve 'impact' returns. Social impact bonds apply a commercial logic to social aims. They may aim to provide housing for those locked out or employment for those who struggle to find a job.

Vanguard Laundry Services in Toowoomba run a social impact business serving the healthcare, aged care, hospitality, accommodation and events industry. Vanguard hires local people keen to return to work after struggling with mental health issues. It stresses jobs and training as its rationale: a social purpose approach to a very competitive industry.

Other social purpose firms provide training and employment for those who are marginalised, for people with physical and learning disabilities, and for those leaving prison. There are an estimated 20,000 such social enterprises across the nation. This is an expanding domain through which Australians can help each other.

Supporting such ventures are emerging capital markets which focus on social enterprise. Investors create pools of capital and look for the right opportunities. The Aspire Social Impact Bond, based in Adelaide, combines reasonable financial returns with an opportunity to help homeless people. By working with established South Australian social housing providers such as Common Ground and Unity Housing, these social impact bonds secure housing outcomes for 600 adults in Adelaide. Safe and stable accommodation emerges everywhere as a prerequisite for breaking cycles of disadvantage.

Social impact investing has attracted government interest with Prime Minister Scott Morrison announcing an expert panel, led by experienced Macquarie Bank investor and founding Chief Executive of Social Ventures Australia, Michael Traill. An interim report from the panel flags initiatives to transform what is described as a 'cottage industry' into a more sophisticated and better understood multi-billion-dollar social impact investing capital market. The report emphasises the appetite of existing social impact investors to invest more.

Drawing particularly on experience from the United Kingdom, the interim report highlights the need for government to be both the enabler and catalyst in creating such a market. There is a pressing need too for intermediaries – people and funds who connect an appetite for more investment with appropriate social purpose enterprises.

As with collective impact, social impact investment also attracts thoughtful critics. Writing in the *Harvard Business Review*, former Chair of Philanthropy Australia Alan Schwartz and co-author Reuben Finighan question the capacity of impact investing, working alone, to address the big problems of our times such as climate change.

To be effective, they argue, social impact investing must change the rules of the game rather than combine charitable purposes with seeking profit. This means government regulation to price externalities created by economic activity; if businesses paid the real cost of pollution as part of their production process, conclude Schwartz and Finighan, then 'all investing becomes impact investing'.

Both the Commonwealth Taskforce and the critique of social impact investing urge partnership; it is hubris for any one sector to believe it has the answers. Charities exist in the shadow of government policy and government, in return, relies on for-purpose organisations to fill significant gaps in social provision.

Working together, charity and government can direct money where it makes a difference, combine talents, encourage social investment and dissolve old assumptions about welfare. The hardest part of change is not embracing new ways but abandoning old ideas. These possess a deadly undertow, dragging us back.

Our responsibility for others remains compelling. The lottery of life means some people will be born and die, whatever their merit and talent, without opportunities for dignity and fulfilment. The measure of justice is whether our society empowers individuals – you, me, everyone – to make meaningful choices, to find the life we value.

Thinking about justice is a spur to practical action. Community leaders across Australia have created important experiments in collective impact. Charities and public agencies can listen to those who must live with the consequences of disadvantage and embrace partnerships for change. Social impact investors add to the stock of capital available to address disadvantage.

In her short story about Omelas, Ursula Le Guin urges us not to shirk moral choices. This is Singer's theme also: to help others within our means is not charity but an obligation.

In striving for justice, charities play a unique role. They can direct effort where it will matter most and make unpopular investments outside the electoral cycle. Journalist Mike Secombe tells us that Australians assume 'in times of crisis – bushfires, floods, droughts, pandemics ... charities will be there to help'. Charities speak to our better selves when they bring in people from the margins. No wonder the Reverend Tim Costello talks of charities as 'the arms and legs' of Australia's safety net.

The randomness of life is with us forever but the outcomes remain our choice.

Australians know this and want to help: look at how enthusiastically we volunteer and donate.

So the challenge is entirely our own. One of the richest societies on the planet stared down a global financial crisis and is now protecting its population from COVID-19. Such a nation can end poverty among its own citizens if it chooses. The effort needs a grand coalition of community, charity and government. We have the model but need the will. For what use is a long and happy life in Omelas if we never face the injustice in our midst?

We start as helpless participants in a blind lottery. Let our beginning not also prove to be our end.

Acknowledgements

With thanks for commissioning and editorial advice to Louise Adler from Hachette, and her colleagues Managing Editor Brigid Mullane and Copy Editor Marisa Wikramanayake.

Thanks also to my employer, the Paul Ramsay Foundation, for support to complete this essay amid a busy program. Foundation Chair Michael Traill and Director Greg Hutchinson provided excellent comments, as did colleagues Jo Taylor, Jeni Whalan and Kris Neill who also managed the project. I appreciate additional textual suggestions and permissions to quote from Peter Beilharz, Robert Dixon, Rory Dufficy, Margaret Gardner, Chris Harrop, Larry Kamener, Conny Lenneberg, Maxine McKew, Abigail Payne, Belinda Probert, Alan Schwartz, Ken Smith, Sian Supski, Howard Whitton and Roger Wilkins. Thanks also to my parents Dolores and Pedr Davis.

References for quotes and statistics cited in *On Life's Lottery* can be found at
https://paulramsayfoundation.org.au

All proceeds from this book have been donated to the St Vincent de Paul Society.

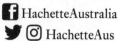

hachette
AUSTRALIA

If you would like to find out more about
Hachette Australia, our authors, upcoming
events and new releases you can visit
our website or our social media channels:

hachette.com.au
HachetteAustralia
HachetteAus